Pocket Positives!

AN A-Z OF INSPIRATIONAL QUOTATIONS

Selected by ALLAN M. NIXON

The Five Mile Press

This is a little book with a big message.

Live by much of the wisdom contained in the following pages and you will be on the way to becoming wealthy and wise. Within these pages some of the world's most successful people pass on their recipes for good living.

Unfortunately most people do not live the fulfilling lives they should.

The aim of this book is to assist you realise your potential through daily positive paragraphs. After all, there is enough negativity around us, so let's get some of the good stuff!

Keep copies of this book handy — it's your passport to a better way of thinking and living. Keep it in your pocket, your purse, glovebox or on your desk. Read it daily. Take time out to close your eyes, breathe slowly and gently relax.

After a while, open your eyes and read for a few minutes, then begin life again as you should — positive.
After all we are only here once.
I dare you to try it — now.

Live and enjoy!

Allan M. Nixon
Bendigo, Victoria
February 1992

ABILITY

God does not ask about your ability.
He asks about your availability.

Anonymous

●

ACHIEVE

Only those who dare to fail greatly can ever achieve greatly.

Robert F. Kennedy (1925-1968)
Former American Senator and Attorney-General

•

Nothing splendid has ever been achieved except by those who dared to believe that something inside them was superior to circumstance.

Bruce Barton

•

ACTION

Action makes more fortunes than caution.

Marquis de Vauvenargues (1715-1747)
French moralist and writer

•

ADVERSITY

There is no education like adversity.

Benjamin Disraeli (1804-1881)
British politician and writer

•

AGE

It's sad to grow old, but nice to ripen.

Brigitte Bardot
French actress

•

Middle age is when you feel on Saturday night the way you used to feel on Monday morning.

F. Rodman

•

ASSETS

One of our main assets is our consistency and uniformity.

Ray Kroc (1902-1984)
Co-founder of McDonalds fast-food restaurants

•

ATTITUDE

Attitudes are more important than facts.

Norman Vincent Peale
American writer and minister

•

A relaxed attitude lengthens a man's life.

Proverbs 14:30

•

Take the attitude of a student. Never be too big to ask questions. Never know too much to learn something new.

Og Mandino
American writer

•

The greatest revolution of our generation is the discovery that human beings, by changing the inner attitudes of their minds, can change the outer aspects of their lives.

William James (1842-1910)
American philosopher and psychologist

•

Attitudes are contagious.

Anonymous

•

B

BEHAVIOUR

Don't copy the behaviour and customs
of this world, but be a new and different
person with a fresh newness in all you
do and think.

Romans 12:2

BEST

There is a better way to do it; find it.

Thomas A. Edison (1847-1931)
American inventor, industrialist and film producer

•

Believe in the best, think your best, study your best, have a goal for your best, never be satisfied with less than your best, try your best, and in the long run things will turn out for the best. Always add up the best.

Henry Ford (1863-1947)
American motor car manufacturer

•

Only mediocrity is always at its best.

Max Beerbohm (1872-1956)
English writer & caricaturist

•

Don't let the best you have done so far
be the standard for the rest of your life.
Gustavus F. Swift (1839-1903)
American meat industry magnate

●

BIG

Do not be afraid to take a big step if
one is required. You can't cross a chasm
in two small jumps.
David Lloyd George (1863-1945)
Former British Prime Minister

●

BOOKS

How many a man has dated a new era in
his life from the reading of a book!
Henry David Thoreau (1817-1862)
American poet, essayist & mystic

●

The effort of attention needed to read a book, and especially a book with serious content, impresses strongly on the memory, so that its ideas can be easily evoked by passing chance and brought into lucky use.

A.H.Z. Carr
American writer

•

It is impossible to mentally or socially enslave a Bible-reading people. The principles of the Bible are the groundwork of human freedom.

Horace Greeley (1811-1872)
American journalist

•

It is impossible to rightly govern the world without God and the Bible.
George Washington (1732-1799)
1st US President, 1789-97

•

The New Testament is the very best book that ever was or ever will be known in the world.
Charles Dickens (1812-1870)
English novelist

•

All that mankind has done, thought, or been is lying in magic preservation in the pages of books.
Thomas Carlyle (1795-1881)
Scottish essayist & historian

BRAIN

The chief purpose of the body is to carry the brain around.
Thomas A. Edison (1847-1931)
American inventor, industrialist, and film producer

•

I not only use all the brains I have, but all I can borrow.
Woodrow Wilson (1856-1925)
28th US President, 1913-21

•

BRAVERY

Bravery is being the only one who knows you're afraid.
Franklin P. Jones (1832-1902)
American capitalist & politician

BRIGHT

No one ever hurt their eyesight by looking at the bright side of life.

Anonymous

•

If you can't see the bright side, polish the dull side.

Anonymous

•

BUSINESS

The secret of business is to know something that nobody else knows.

Aristotle Socrates Onassis (1906-1975)
Greek shipping magnate

•

CHARACTER

A man never discloses his own character so clearly as when he describes another's.

Jean Paul Friedrich Richter (1763-1826)
German writer

Character consists of what you do on the third and fourth tries.
James A. Michener
American writer

•

CHARITY

With malice toward none, with charity for all.
Abraham Lincoln (1809-1865)
16th US President, 1861-65

•

CONCENTRATE

Concentration is my motto.
First honesty, then industry,
then concentration.
Andrew Carnegie (1835-1919)
Scottish-American industrialist & philanthropist

•

CONTROL

If your aim is control, it must be self-control first. If your aim is management, it must be self-management first.

Anonymous

•

COURAGE

One man with courage makes a majority.

Andrew Jackson (1767-1845)
7th US President, 1829-37

•

D

DECISION

You don't drown by falling in the water.
You drown by staying there.

Anonymous

DEEDS

By his deeds we know a man.
African proverb

•

DESTINATION

Knowing your destination is half the journey.
Anonymous

•

What you get by reaching your destination isn't nearly as important as what you become by reaching that destination.

Zig Ziglar
American writer and motivational speaker

•

DESTINY

Destiny is not a matter of chance, it is a matter of choice.

William Jennings Bryan

•

DETERMINE

Determine on some course, more than a wild exposure to each chance.

William Shakespeare (1564-1616)
English dramatist & poet

•

DIRECTION

I can't change the direction of the wind. But I can adjust my sails.

Anonymous

•

DISCIPLINE

Discipline is the soul of an army.
It makes small numbers formidable,
procures success to the weak, and
esteem to all.

George Washington (1732-1799)
1st US President, 1789-97

•

The discipline of writing something
down is the first step toward
making it happen.

Lee Iacocca
American writer and automobile executive

•

DREAMS

All big men are dreamers.
They see things in the soft haze of
a spring day or in the red fire of a long
winter's evening.
Some of us let great dreams die, but
others nourish and protect them, nurse
them through bad days till they bring
them to the sunshine and light which
comes always to those who sincerely
hope that their dreams will come true.

Woodrow Wilson (1856-1925)
28th US President, 1913-21

Some men see things as they are and say 'Why?'
I dream things that never were, and say, 'Why not'?

George Bernard Shaw (1856-1950)
Anglo-Irish dramatist & critic.

●

All men who have achieved great things have been dreamers.

Orison Swett Marden

●

DURABLE

The more I study the world, the more I am convinced of the inability of brute force to create anything durable.

Napoleon Bonaparte I (1769-1821)
French emperor

●

ENTHUSIASM

Nothing great was ever achieved without enthusiasm.

Ralph Waldo Emerson (1803-1882)
American essayist, poet & abolitionist

●

None so old as those who have outlived enthusiasm.

Henry David Thoreau (1817-1862)
American poet, essayist & mystic

•

If you are not getting as much from life as you want to, then examine the state of your enthusiasm.

Norman Vincent Peale
American writer & minister

•

Enthusiasm without knowledge is no good; impatience will get you into trouble.

Proverbs 19:2

•

The person who loves always becomes enthusiastic.

Norman Vincent Peale
American writer & minister

•

Act enthusiastic and you become enthusiastic.

Dale Carnegie
American writer, educationist & motivator

•

You can do anything if you have enthusiasm... Enthusiasm is at the bottom of all progress. With it, there is accomplishment. Without it, there are only alibis.

Henry Ford (1863-1947)
American motor car manufacturer.

•

A positive attitude triggers enthusiasm.
Elwood N. Chapman
American writer

•

No man who is enthusiastic about his work has anything to fear from life.
Samuel Goldwyn (1882-1974)
American film producer

•

EXCELLENCE

Excellence is to do a common thing in an uncommon way.
Booker T. Washington (1856-1915)
American educationalist

•

EXERCISE

The best exercise for the heart is to lean over backwards for somebody else.

Anonymous

•

EXPERIENCE

You gain strength, courage, and confidence by every experience by which you really stop to look fear in the face.

Eleanor Roosevelt (1884-1962)
Former First Lady of the United States, 1933-45

•

Experience is a hard teacher because she gives the test first, the lesson afterwards.

Vernon Sanders Law

•

The art of living is the art of using experience " your own and other people's.

Viscount Samuel (1870-1963)
British politician & administrator

•

EXTRAORDINARY

The difference between ordinary and extraordinary is that little extra.

Anonymous

•

FATE

Whatever fate befalls you, do not give way to great rejoicing, or great lamentation ... All things are full of change, and your fortunes may turn at any moment.

Arthur Schopenhauer (1788-1860)
Philosopher of metaphysics

●

FEAR

Fear is never a reason for quitting:
it is only an excuse.

Norman Vincent Peale
American writer & minister

•

FORGIVENESS

Forgive your enemies, but never forget
their names.

John F. Kennedy (1917-1963)
35th US President, 1961-63

FRIENDS

My best friend is the one who brings out the best in me.

Henry Ford (1863-1947)
American motor car manufacturer

●

Am I not destroying my enemies when I make friends of them ?

Abraham Lincoln (1809-1865)
16th US President, 1861-65

●

Friendship is tested in the thick years of success rather than in the thin years of struggle.

Barry Humphries
Australian humorist, writer and actor

●

A man who turns his back on his friends soon finds himself facing a very small audience.
Dick Powell (1904-1963)
American actor

●

It is easier to forgive an enemy than a friend.
Aystin O'Malley

●

G

GENIUS

Genius is infinite painstaking.
Henry Wadsworth Longfellow (1807-1882)
American poet

•

Genius is one per cent inspiration and ninety-nine per cent perspiration.
Thomas A. Edison (1847-1931)
American inventor, film producer and industrialist

•

GOALS

All successful people have a goal.
No one can get anywhere unless he
knows where he wants to go and what
he wants to be or do.

Norman Vincent Peale
American writer & minister

•

A man without a purpose is like a ship
without a rudder.

Thomas Carlyle (1795-1881)
Scottish-American industrialist and philanthropist

•

This one step — choosing a goal and
sticking to it — changes everything.

Scott Reid

•

GREAT

There is a great man, who makes every man feel small. But the real great man is the man who makes every man feel great.

G.K. Chesteron (1874-1936)
English fiction writer and critic

●

GROWTH

Love seems the swiftest, but it is the slowest of all growths. No man or woman really knows what perfect love is until they have been married for a quarter of a century.

Mark Twain (1835-1910)
American writer & humorist

●

H

HAPPINESS

Happiness lies in the joy of achievement
and the thrill of creative effort.

Franklin D. Roosevelt (1882-1945)
32nd US President, 1933-45

●

Action may not always bring happiness, but there is no happiness without action.
Benjamin Disraeli (1804-1881)
British politician & writer

●

Knowledge of what is possible is the beginning of happiness.
George Santayana (1863-1952)
Spanish-American philosopher & poet

●

The secret of happiness is not in doing what one likes, but in liking what one does.
James A. Barrie

●

Happiness doesn't depend on the actual number of blessings we manage to scratch from life, only our attitude towards them.

Alexander Solzhenitsyn
Russian writer & former dissident

•

HEALTH

These new wonder drugs are so powerful that you have to be in perfect health to take them.

Bob Hope
British-American actor and comedian

•

HISTORY

Men make their own history more wisely when they know what that history has been about.

Manning Clark (1915-1991)
Australian historian, university professor and writer

•

HONESTY

We will keep the bastards honest.

Don Chipp
Australian Democrats politician
(On the role of his party in the 1980 federal election.)

•

HOPE

There are no hopeless situations; there are only men who have grown hopeless about them.

Clare Booth Luce (1903-1987)
American playwright

●

Hope deferred maketh the heart sick.
Proverbs 13:12

●

I

IDEA
An idea isn't responsible for the
people who believe in it.
Don Marquis

•

IMPRESSION
You never get a second chance to make
a good first impression.
Anonymous

•

Every man is a hero and an oracle to somebody, and to that person, whatever he says has an enhanced value.

Ralph Waldo Emerson (1803-1882)
American essayist & poet

J

JOY

May your joys be as deep as the ocean, your sorrows as light as its foam.

Anonymous

JUSTICE

Though the sword of justice is sharp, it
will not slay the innocent.
Chinese proverb

•

JOURNEY

A journey of a thousand miles begins
with a single step.
Anonymous

•

Success is a journey not a destination.
Ben Sweetland

•

Knowledge is of two kinds. We know a subject ourselves, or we know where to find information on it.
Samuel Johnson (1709-1784)
English writer

•

Knowledge is power.
Francis Bacon (1561-1626)
English lawyer, scientist, essayist & philosopher

•

To be conscious that you are ignorant is a great step to knowledge.
Benjamin Disraeli (1804-1881)
British politician and writer

•

L

LEADER

I learned that a great leader is a man who has the ability to get other people to do what they don't want to do and like it.

Harry S. Truman (1884-1972)
33rd US President, 1945-52
(Responsible authority for the dropping of the atom bomb on Japan)

Leadership: the art of getting someone else to do something you want done because he wants to do it,

Dwight D. Eisenhower (1890-1969)
34th US President, 1953-61

•

The great difference between the real leader and the pretender is — that the one sees into the future, while the other regards only the present; the one lives by the day, and acts on expediency; the other acts on enduring principles and for immortality.

Edmund Burke (1729-1797)
British politician & writer

•

LIBERTY

The tree of liberty must be refreshed from time to time with the blood of patriots and tyrants. It is its natural manure.

Thomas Jefferson (1743-1826)
3rd US President, 1801-09

●

Liberty, when it begins to take root, is a plant of rapid growth.

George Washington (1732-1799)
1st US President, 1789-97

●

LIFE

Long life is the reward of the righteous; grey hair is the glorious crown.

Proverbs 16:31

●

Decide carefully, exactly what you want
in life, then work like mad to make sure
you get it!
Hector Crawford (1913-1991)
Australian TV Producer

●

Life is either a daring adventure or
nothing.
Helen Keller (1880-1968)
American blind and deaf writer

●

Live every day as though it's your last.
One day you'll get it right!
Zig Ziglar
American writer and motivational speaker

●

LOVE

By love serve one another.
Galatians 5:13

Men and women are made to love each other. It's only by loving each other that they can achieve anything.
Christina Stead (1902-1983)
Australian writer

I know of only one duty, and that is to love.
Albert Camus (1913-1960)
French writer and actor

You can give without loving, but you can't love without giving.
Oswald J. Smith

•

God doesn't look at how much we do, but with how much love we do it.
Mother Theresa
Relief worker in the Third-World

•

LUCK

Anyone who does not know how to make the most of his luck has no right to complain if it passes him by.
Miguel de Saavedra Cervantes (1547-1832)
Spanish novelist; author of Don Quixote

•

M

MIND

Man's mind, once stretched by a new idea, never regains its original dimensions.

Oliver Wendell Holmes (1809-1984)
American writer & physician

●

Luck favours the mind that is prepared.

Louis Pasteur (1822-1895)
French bacteriologist

●

The immature mind hops from one thing to another; the mature mind seeks to follow through.

Harry A. Overstreet
American writer

•

MONEY

Money is like an arm or leg — use it or lose it.

Henry Ford (1863-1947)
American motor car manufacturer

•

Some people pretend to be rich, but have nothing. Others pretend to be poor, but own a fortune.

Proverbs 13:7

•

If money is your hope for independence you will never have it. The only real security that a man can have in this world is a reserve of knowledge, experience and ability.
Henry Ford (1863-1947)
American motor car manufacturer

•

Money can buy everything except the things we want and need the most.
G.L. Robertson

•

Money makes money, and the money money makes, makes more money.
Benjamin Franklin (1706-1790)
American statesman & scientist.

•

N

NEGOTIATE

Let us never negotiate out of fear, but let us never fear to negotiate.

John Fitzgerald Kennedy (1917-1963)
35th US President, 1961-63

•

O

OPPORTUNITY

Failure is only the opportunity to begin
again more intelligently.
Henry Ford (1863-1947)
American motor car manufacturer

•

If heaven drops a date, open your mouth.
Chinese proverb

•

P

PATRIOTISM

I love God and my country; I honour the flag; I will serve the King, and cheerfully obey my parents, teachers, and the laws.

Victorian Education Gazette,
October 1901, suppl. 2
(Oath of allegiance used in Victorian State Primary Schools.)

●

We swear by the Southern Cross to stand truly by each other, and fight to defend our rights and liberties.
Peter Lalor (1827-1889)
Australian politician and Eureka Stockade rebel
(Oath taken by Lalor and his volunteers prior to the Eureka Stockade rebellion.)

•

PEACE

You will give yourself peace of mind if you do every act of your life as if it were your last.
Marcus Aurelius (121-180 AD)
Roman emperor and philosopher

•

PLAN

Plan your work and work your plan.
Norman Vincent Peale
American writer & minister

•

Plan for the future because that's where you are going to spend the rest of your life.
Mark Twain (1835-1910)
American writer & humorist

•

Any enterprise built by wise planning becomes strong through common sense, and profits wonderfully by keeping abreast of the facts.
Proverbs 24:3-4

•

We may make our plans, but God has the last word.
Proverbs 16:1

●

PLEASURE

Many a man thinks he is buying pleasure, when he is really selling himself to it.

Benjamin Franklin (1706-1790)
American statesman and scientist

●

QUALITY

Quality is never an accident; it is always the result of high intention, sincere effort, intelligent direction, and skillful execution; it represents the wise choice of many alternatives.

Willa A. Foster

QUIET

When you become quiet, it just dawns on you.

Thomas A. Edison (1847-1931)
American inventor, film producer and industrialist

R

REPUTATION

The only time you realise you have a reputation is when you fail to live up to it.

Anonymous

REVOLUTION

The surest guide to the correctness of the path that women take is 'joy in the struggle'. Revolution is the festival of the oppressed.

Germaine Greer
Australian writer and feminist

•

RIGHT

I must stand with anybody that stands right, stand with him while he is right, and part with him when he goes wrong.

Abraham Lincoln (1809-1865)
16th US President, 1861-65

•

Whether you believe you can do a thing
or believe you can't, you are right.
Henry Ford (1863-1947)
American motor car manufacturer

S

SAFETY

The desire for safety stands against
every great and noble enterprise.
Publius Cornelius Tacitus (55-120 AD)
Roman historian

It is always safe to learn, even from our enemies; seldom safe to venture to instruct, even our friends.
Chas C. Colton (1780-1832)
English writer

•

SELF-IMAGE

No one can make you feel inferior without your consent.
Eleanor Roosevelt (1884-1962)
Former First Lady of the United States, 1933-45

•

Self criticism is a luxury all politicians should indulge in, but it is best done in private.
Malcolm Fraser
Former Australian Prime Minister, 1975-1983

•

SMILES

There is no other weapon in the whole female armory to which men are so vulnerable as they are to a smile.

Dorothy Dix
American writer

•

SOLUTION

Every problem contains the seeds of its own solution.

Stanley Arnold

•

Things should be made as simple as possible, but not simpler.

Albert Einstein (1879-1965)
German-Swiss-American theoretical physicist

•

STRENGTH

This stuff about the meek inheriting the earth is a load of bullshit. The weak need the strong to look after them.
Bob Hawke
Former Australian Prime Minister, 1983-1991

•

You must be the anvil or the hammer.
Johann Wolfgang von Goethe (1749-1832)
German poet & dramatist

•

I'm grateful for all my problems. As each of them was overcome I became stronger and more able to meet those yet to come. I grew on my difficulties.
J.C. Penney (1875-1971)
American retailing magnate

•

I could do nothing without problems, they toughen my mind. In fact I tell my assistants not to bring me their successes for they weaken me; but rather to bring me their problems, for they strengthen me.

Charles F. Kettering (1876-1968)
American engineer & inventor

•

Be strong and courageous, and do the work.

1 Chronicles 28:20

•

The world breaks everyone and afterwards many are strong at the broken places.

Ernest Hemingway (1899-1961)
American novelist

SUCCESS

Singleness of purpose is one of the chief essentials for success in life, no matter what may be one's aim.

John D. Rockefeller, Jr. (1874-1960)
Philanthropist

●

I never allow any difficulties. The great secret of being useful and successful is to admit of no difficulties.

Sir George Gipps (1791-1847)
Governor of Victoria

●

Success is the maximum utilization of the ability that you have.
Zig Ziglar
American writer and motivational speaker

•

No man fails who does his best.
Orison Swett Marden

•

TALK

There are only two kinds of people to talk things over with.
People who have done what you want to do and those who have paid the price you want to pay.

Charles Jones
American businessman, motivator

To talk is our chief business in this world, and talk is by far the most accessible pleasure. It costs nothing in money; it is all profit, it completes education, founds and fosters friendships, and can be enjoyed at any age and in almost any state of health.

Robert Louis Stevenson (1850-1894)
Scottish novelist, poet & essayist

•

TIME

Time is like a precious jewel. It must be guarded well and worn with discretion or you will suddenly realise that it has been stolen.

Glenn Bland
American businessman and writer

•

Time management ... is one of the most important keys to your success. But it is only a key. Before you can use that key you have to be motivated; and before that can happen you have to find out what a terrific and wonderful person you really are.

Rita Davenport
American time management consultant, writer and TV show host

•

Don't serve time, make time serve you,
*** Willie Sutton (1860-1928)***
American educationalist

●

Doest thou love life? Then do not squander time; for that's the stuff life is made of.
Benjamin Franklin (1706-1790)
American statesman & scientist

●

These trying times are the good old days we'll be longing for in a few years.

Jose Ferrer

●

Your time is limited, but your imagination is not.
Van Crouch
American writer and motivational speaker

●

U

UNITY

The unity of man is based upon his infinite diversity.

Vance Palmer (1885-1959)
Australian writer

UNIQUE

All cases are unique, and very similar to others.

T.S. Eliot (1888-1965)
Anglo-American poet, critic & playwright.

•

UP

If you fell down yesterday, stand up today.

H.G. Wells (1866-1946)
English novelist and teacher

•

V

VIRTUE

It has been my experience that folks who have no vices have very few virtues.

Abraham Lincoln (1809-1865)
16th US President, 1861-65

•

W

WEALTH

Lazy men are soon poor; hard workers get rich.
Proverbs 10:4

•

Wealth is a good servant, a very bad mistress.
Anonymous

•

WINNING

An integral part of being a star is having the will to win. All the champions have it.

Betty Cuthbert
Australian Olympic gold-medal sprinter

●

Winners are not people without any problems. Winners are people who have learned how to overcome their problems.

Mike Murdock

●

Winning isn't everything, but wanting to win is.

Vince Lombardi
American football coach

●

WISDOM

I don't think much of a man who is not wiser today than he was yesterday.

Abraham Lincoln (1809-1865)
16th US President, 1861-65

●

The teachings of the wise are a fountain of life; they will help you escape when your life is in danger.

Proverbs 13:14

●

The foolish man wonders at the unusual, but the wise man at the usual.

Ralph Waldo Emerson (1803-1882)
American essayist, poet & abolitionist

●

Be with wise men and become wise.
Proverbs 13:20

•

The wisdom of the wise, and the experience of the ages, may be preserved by quotations.
Isaac Disraeli (1766-1848)
English literary critic, pioneer of literary research

•

WORDS

Man does not live by words alone, despite the fact that sometimes he has to eat them.

Broderick Crawford
American actor

•

Words should be employed as a means,
not as an end;
language is the instrument, conviction is
the work.

Sir Joshua Reynolds (1723-1792)
English painter

•

WORK

To my mind the best investment a
young man starting out in business
could possibly make is to give all his
time, all his energies to work, just plain,
hard work.

Charles M. Schwab (1862-1939)
American industrialist

•

The glory of a workman, still more of a master-workman, that he does his work well, ought to be his most precious possession; like the 'honour of a soldier', dearer to him than life.

Thomas Carlyle (1795-1881)
Scottish-American industrialist & philanthropist

●

It is impossible to enjoy idling thoroughly unless one has plenty of work to do.

Jerome Jerome (1859-1927)
English playwright & humorist

●

Always work with the end results in mind.
Rita Davenport
American time management consultant, writer and TV show host.

●

The force, the mass of character, mind, heart or soul that a man can put into any work, is the most important factor in that work.
A. P. Peabody (1811-1893)
American writer

●

The highest reward for man's toil is not what he gets for it but what he becomes by it.
John Ruskin (1819-1900)
English writer & critic

●

Y

YES

Where we are free to act, we are free to refrain from acting, and where we are able to say no, we are also able to say yes.

Aristotle (384-322 BC)
Greek philospher

●

Z

ZEST

Zest is the secret of all beauty. There is no beauty that is attractive without zest.

Christian Dior
French couturier